A Cat's Tale

A Story of
Redemption

T.A. Alexander

Written Words Publishing LLC
P.O. Box 462622
Aurora, Colorado 80046
www.writtenwordspublishing.com

Published by Written Words Publishing LLC May 8, 2025.

ISBN: 978-1-961610-37-8 (paperback)
ISBN: 978-1-961610-38-5 (hardcover)

Library of Congress Control Number: 2025908285

Cover designed by T.A. Alexander

Illustrations created by T.A. Alexander using BookBildr. All images are used under license and permission from BookBildr.

Manufactured and printed in the United States of America

This book is dedicated to those who work and sacrifice tirelessly for all of God's creation: serving the broken, finding the lost, healing the wounded, and providing a safe space where hope and love bring the restoration that forever changes lives.

-and-

In loving memory of my big brother who always understood.

"Through many dangers, toils, and snares, I Have already come: 'Tis grace has brought Me safe thus far, And grace will lead me home."
—John Newton

There's a place I go when I need to see clearly,
It's sunlit and warm, this place I love dearly.
My window, my basket, the sun so bright,
Yet, I still recall so many cold nights...

I've grown in this place I call my home,
Brought here as a kitten, to call my own.
The memories I have of the life I once knew,
Seem to fade with age, but there remain a few.

So, my story to tell, I often am told,
To all with soft hearts, never grows old.
Through difficult times, through all the strife,
Love carried me home, love brought me to life!

I was born a kitten to a mother of four,
We were one of many litters she bore.
Different colors, yet mom was all white,
Ambling around, we made quite a sight.

An odd assortment we kittens so small,
We always ran to mother's sweet call.
We had a good life or so we thought,
With food, love and the mice that she caught!

Our home in a shed was warm in the hay,
Cozy and bright and that's where we'd play.
Close to mother we'd cuddle and sing,
We loved all the bugs and crickets she'd bring.

As the days passed by and though we were small,
I'll never forget when it changed for us all.
Storming outside, the wind began blowing,
It blew so hard and it soon began snowing!

Bitterly cold, curled tight in a ball,
The five of us slept, unaware of it all.
And while we lay sleeping, feeling quite safe,
The shed door creaked open, revealing a face.

A man came in, I know I'd seen him before,
He owned the big house that was just next door.
Big and quiet, he glanced all around,
And saw us all sleeping in a big fluffy mound.

Slowly, he moved to gather some things,
A box, a blanket and a long piece of string.
Awakening quickly to all the noise,
Stretching and yawning, he brought us all toys!

We played with the string he dangled before us,
Chasing it round, mewing in chorus.
What a great game, oh what great fun!
If we'd only known then, we should've run.

Masterfully planned, he knelt to the ground,
Collected us each as we all raced around.
Placed all of us youngsters inside of a box,
Unaware that our mother helplessly watched.

He put the box in a truck, the engine he started,
Slowly he drove 'til the road soon parted.
Past a pond and a light post, past houses and trees,
Oh, won't he stop, it's so hard to see!

He drove and he drove, past the river we went,
Around the corners, until he was spent.
He came to a halt on top of a hill,
He opened the door and we felt the cold chill.

We could see from our box with the limited view,
We would not return to the home we once knew.
It must have been good, it must have been right,
This place where he left us, so far out of sight.

Why he lifted us gently in the palm of his hand,
Is something so odd, I don't understand.
Sad and confused, we didn't make a sound,
As our paws so lightly touched the cold ground.

After starting the truck, the man drove away,
As we watched him leave, we started to pray,
"Bring him back to us soon, this is all a mistake,
To leave us alone on this road by the lake!"

No shelter, no food, no comfort in sight,
What do we do in our sad lonely plight?
What do we do now that we're all alone?
How to find warmth in the cold of the stones?

There were too many lessons still to be taught,
By our mom, how to catch all the mice that she caught.
We still needed her and her care to grow strong,
Could it be he didn't know what he did was so wrong?

After scrambling through bushes in panic and fear,
We had to find cover and somewhere quite near!
We were hungry and tired and with all of our might,
Looked for shelter in what little remained of the light.

As the cold drew upon us, we laid down to rest,
We soon became sleepy, remembering mom best,
When she'd purr words of comfort to quiet our fear:
"Be strong, of good courage and let love draw near!"

With her strong words to guide us, we fell deep to sleep,
Knowing somehow with faith our lives we would keep.
Night turned to day and the sun shined so bright,
Somehow, I believed we would all be alright!

We scavenged for food by night and by day,
Sometimes, we'd nap and often we'd play!
After all, we were kittens still young and so small,
Being left behind was not the end of it all!

Sometimes, I'd think of our home far away,
Where would mom be, if she was okay…
And though we survived, would we ever be safe,
Would we someday find our way out of this place?

And as if in answer to a prayer softly said,
I dreamed of a home with a big warm bed!
With room for us all, my siblings and I,
Where we'd not be beneath the cold night sky.

Then one day soon after came a lady in blue,
Calling and calling, we hadn't a clue.
What did she want and why was she here?
Her purpose to us just wasn't quite clear.

She came every day, right before dark,
Her old rusty truck, she'd pull into park.
She'd empty her bag in a heap on the ground,
And after she'd leave, we'd go sniff around.

Day after day, this kind lady would come,
She'd sit by a tree and quietly hum.
Softly encouraging us to draw near,
Her voice was so soft, our hearts held no fear.

We soon discovered she meant us no harm,
Her strange gentle way was part of her charm.
We became bolder as the days made us brave,
It was touch and warm places we started to crave.

This lady, she showed us her lap was quite safe,
We'd sit and purr while she spoke of her place.
She told us of wonders we had yet to know…
Warm fuzzies and baskets and fires aglow!

She had a house large, with room for us all,
If we'd only trust her and come to her call.
The four of us were curious and yet, being shy,
How could we know what she told us weren't lies?

It's hard to believe when you've known so little,
One's faith and hope can grow quite brittle.
But we all took a gamble, we trusted in fate,
Went home with the lady and still to this date...

We sleep in our baskets, warm with the sun.
The view from our windows is wonderfully fun.
We're plump and round, our coats how they glisten!
It's important now that you all will listen...

Because the story I tell is of love, not fear.
The view from our baskets is really quite clear,
To hope and to risk is the message I give,
In shelter and love, one learns how to live.

The reward of love is to grow true and strong,
Step out of fear, right what is wrong.
I hope you will know the truth which I speak,
It is love after all, we all need and seek.

So, extend yourself out to those who have need,
Whether four legs or two, it's all in the deed.
It is love that's the gift and after all...
We are all intertwined, big and small!

Because the story I tell is of love, not fear.
The view from our baskets is really quite clear,
To hope and to risk is the message I give,
In shelter and love, one learns how to live.

The reward of love is to grow true and strong,
Step out of fear, right what is wrong.
I hope you will know the truth which I speak,
It is love after all, we all need and seek.

So, extend yourself out to those who have need,
Whether four legs or two, it's all in the deed.
It is love that's the gift and after all...
We are all intertwined, big and small!